A Cookie to Celebrate

Published by Mango Publishing Group, a division of Mango Media Inc.

Cover, Layout & Design: Morgane Leoni
Stylist: Amy Beiser
Photographer: Jennifer Schaaf

For permission requests, please contact the publisher at:

Mango Publishing Group
2850 Douglas Road, 3rd Floor
Coral Gables, FL 33134 U.S.A.
info@mango.bz

For special orders, quantity sales, course adoptions and corporate sales, please email the publisher at sales@mango.bz. For trade and wholesale sales, please contact Ingram Publisher Services at: customer.service@ingramcontent.com or +1.800.509.4887.

A Cookie to Celebrate: Recipes and Decorating Tips for Everyday Baking and Holidays

Library of Congress Cataloging
SBN: (p) 978-1-63353-756-9, (e) 978-1-63353-757-6
ry of Congress Control Number: 2018940705
ING / Courses & Dishes / Cookies

States of America

A Cookie to Celebrate

Recipes and Decorating Tips for Everyday Baking and Holidays

Jana Douglass

Mango Publishing
CORAL GABLES

Contents

Introduction

Everyone Celebrating with Cookies!

I was in my early twenties, weeks away from holding a college degree in my hands, with no job lined up. Cue the stress baking. Sound familiar? I pulled my grandmother's sugar cookie recipe out of my beloved recipe book and slaved over cookies for my own graduation dinner. They were awful. The text was piped so badly you couldn't even tell which school I had graduated from, and I'm surprised everyone left the dinner with all their teeth! But there was one thing that always stuck with me: *cookies bring people joy*. Those attending my graduation dinner didn't care that the lines weren't straight or that the texture was off. From then on, I was hooked.

I spent the next nine months giving all my spare time to baking and, like a true millennial, humbly bragging about my new set of skills on social media. My cookies evolved from an unattractive mess with cavity-inducing icing to photo-ready designs that are so tasty you won't even think twice about digging in.

A business was born: I had gained a humbling number of followers (anyone else do a happy dance when you hit 1,000?!) and, most importantly, had enough clients to take a crack at pursuing my passion full time. I've never looked back. It hasn't always been the easiest, or as happy as my Instagram feed might make it seem, but I have kept going, bringing JOY into people's lives one cookie at a time. People choose to include my cookies in life's biggest and most special moments; I mean, how cool is that?!

Jana Lee's Bake Shop is my baby. I spent more time curating the brand's name than the majority of expectant parents spend awaiting their new child. I turned to the internet to find artistic talent to make a logo, with one requirement that I know will shock you: it had to be pink! I found the best bakery boxes, made my own website, and took on my first clients who weren't friends with my mom. I was emailing and working by day and baking and decorating by night out of my one tiny oven. At this point, I was personally hand delivering every single cookie, mostly because I was afraid of the internet and giving out my address, but I also knew quality and service mattered! I didn't have a storefront, so the extra cost of perfect packaging and the added headache of fighting traffic was worth it. Almost immediately after opening for business and being overwhelmed by orders, I started the process of building my own commercial kitchen. Within five months, Jana Lee's Bake Shop had a new home. It wasn't fancy, it could have been prettier, but it did the trick and has gotten us to where we are today. I'm writing to all of you in the middle of designing a bigger and much prettier home for Jana Lee's Bake Shop, and let me tell you, this is all pretty surreal.

Before we dive into the cookies, the real reason you're all here, I have a few things for you to keep in mind. I am not a professionally trained baker. I do not have an art background. I had never even set foot in a commercial kitchen until I built my *own*. This book is my self-taught knowledge, creativity, and skills, all fueled by my passion for entrepreneurship.

I hope this book provides you with a new skill, a fun activity, and an excuse to celebrate. Remember, your friends don't care if Santa's hat turned out more pink than red, no one will notice that your ruffles look like an intentional blob, and a misspelling can provide a few laughs—trust me, it happens! I have burned, dropped, and misspelled more cookies than you can count. The best part about "messing up"? The evidence gets eaten!

Life is short, have a cookie to celebrate!!

Chapter 1

Cookie Base

This chapter is quite literally about how to create the base for all of your decorated cookies! It is super important, because what's the point of celebrating with a cookie if it doesn't taste good? This might be your favorite chapter or possibly your worst enemy depending on the set of skills you're working with, but I can guarantee you will be referring back to this chapter the most! Grab your measuring spoons and buckle up—it's time to bake! Like I said before, I am not professionally trained. The tips and tricks you will read in this chapter work for me, and it's okay if you prefer something different; I encourage it! There are so many talented bakers willing to share their knowledge, I suggest hopping on social media and soaking it all in until you find the right equation for *you*!

This is a standard recipe for soft cut-out cookies. I suggest using the highest quality ingredients that are available to you. Take the time to test different extracts based on your personal preference. Almond extract is a simple yet delicious substitute for vanilla!

Cut-Out Sugar Cookies

INGREDIENTS

- 2 c. salted butter (room temperature)
- 2 ½ c. sugar
- 2 large eggs
- 4 tsp. vanilla extract
- 6 c. flour
- 1 tsp. baking powder
- 1 tsp. salt
- Airtight container, for storage

DIRECTIONS

1. Preheat the oven to 350 degrees F.
2. In a standing mixer, cream together the butter and sugar until fluffy. Add the eggs and vanilla, then stir until combined.
3. In a separate bowl, combine the flour, baking powder, and salt. While the mixer is on low, slowly add the flour mixture until just combined. The dough

should be pulling away from the sides of the mixer. At this point, wrap the dough in plastic wrap and let chill for about 30 minutes.

4. Sprinkle powdered sugar so the dough doesn't stick, and roll out the dough to about ⅜ inch. Don't be afraid to get a ruler so you can visually see what ⅜ of an inch looks like. We love thick cookies!
5. Using your desired shapes, cut out the dough. Make the most out of the rolled dough by cutting out the shapes as close to each other as possible.
6. Place the dough on a parchment lined baking sheet and bake to perfection for 8–10 minutes or until the center of the cookie has risen and is puffy.
7. Let the cookies cool on the cookie sheet until completely cool to the touch. Repeat these steps until all your cookies are baked!

Yields 3–4 dozen cookies.

The dough can be stored tightly wrapped in your refrigerator for up to one week. Once the cookies are baked, store in an airtight container until you are ready to decorate.

•

Now, I'm sure you have some sort of collection of cookie cutters collecting dust in a lost drawer in the kitchen, or like my mom, maybe you keep them packed away with the Christmas decorations, pulling them out only when Santa is coming to town. Pull them out and see what you're working with! So many shapes can be repurposed into other things; don't be afraid to sketch things out if you can't figure out what the shape is supposed to be, trust me, it happens!

For this book I used a variety of Ann Clark Cutters; they are metal and made right here in the USA. The following is not just a list of cutters used in the book, this set is a perfect assortment to start your own cutter collection:

- Circle
- Heart
- Ice cream cone
- Rectangle
- Basket
- Pumpkin

- Snowflake
- Ring
- Onesie
- Santa and a cake

Now this is only the beginning; there are so many amazing cookie cutter companies and more and more are popping up each day with the powers of 3D printing. Do a little research and support a small business! I'm sure if you follow us on social media you have seen our huge pegboard we use to store all of the hundreds of cutters we own. Try keeping that organized! Make sure to properly clean your cutters before and after each use.

Voilà! Your blank cookies are ready for all your artistic skills. Bookmark this chapter because you will be using this recipe a lot. Don't be afraid to try other recipes or other flavors, or just adding extra flair to this one. Troubleshoot your family recipe; I tend to find older cookie recipes call for cookies to be rolled too thin and baked too long, but both are easy fixes! Honestly, I won't blame you if this is your least favorite chapter. Baking isn't for everyone! Coming from someone who would beg my very sweet now-fiancé to make all my cookie dough for me, I get it! My joy comes from decorating. Find your joy!

Take the time to
turn off your mixer
and scrape the sides of the
bowl clean of any ingredients.
Make sure nothing has
settled at the bottom of
the bowl.

PS: No one ever said you can't bake and decorate pre-made cookie dough! Pick your battles and find a frozen dough that doesn't spread too much.

Notes

- For those looking for cookies that are precisely the same thickness every time, consider purchasing dough guides. These are typically plastic rods that take the guesswork out of rolling! I highly suggest them for people planning to bake a lot of cookies.
- To keep cookies soft and maintain a consistent texture, I do not recommend rolling out the dough more than six times. This is why it is important to make the most out of your dough when cutting it out! Think of it like a puzzle.
- With this recipe, the cookies *will* spread in the oven but should hold their general shape.

Chapter 2

Royal Icing

ProGel
Pink
Professional Grade

Royal icing is the key to perfectly decorated cookies. It is also the hardest part to master! This chapter will guide you through the step-by-step process of making royal icing, how to achieve the perfect colors, and the biggest challenge: the consistency! Royal icing dries completely hard, which makes the cookies easy to package without a mess.

This is a standard royal icing recipe using meringue powder. I prefer to use meringue powder as a safety precaution with the volume of cookies I make and decorate. If this is the method you would like to use, I would highly suggest ordering meringue powder from a specialty baking store. Picking up this ingredient from a local craft store may cause some problems and affect the overall taste of the cookies. If you're not looking to invest in a container of meringue powder just yet, feel free to utilize a traditional royal icing recipe using egg whites. All of the same principles you will learn in later sections will apply exactly the same if you choose to use egg whites; however, you will need to find your own royal icing recipe, since a simple egg white substitution in this recipe will not have the results you expect.

Notice how the icing is holding a stiff shape. When the paddle is pulling out of the bowl, a stiff peak should form. This is when your shiny bright white icing is done.

Royal Icing

INGREDIENTS

- 4 lbs. powdered sugar
- 1 c. meringue powder
- ¾ c. water
- 4 T. vanilla
- Airtight container, for storage

DIRECTIONS

1. Combine all ingredients in the bowl of a standing mixer. Use a PADDLE attachment, this trick will help you later on while decorating. A whisk attachment creates more air in your icing, which leads to frustrating bubbles later in the process. Please trust me, give your whisk attachment a break and use the paddle!
2. Slowly mix the ingredients until combined, turning the mixer up to a medium speed. Keep an eye out for the sludge-like mix to brighten into white icing

as mixing creates stiff peaks; this process takes a while, so be patient. Time varies by mixer, but expect to be whipping for about 10 minutes.

3. To test the peaks, pull the paddle out of the bowl; the icing should be stiff and create a steady peak both in the bowl of icing and coming off the paddle. Cover immediately or transfer to an airtight container.

4. There are some troubles you might run into; over-whipping your icing is a real problem! The icing might appear to be okay, but then when you go to ice the cookies, the icing will never dry. Keep an eye on your mixer—a watched mixer *does* create the perfect peaks! As soon as you see those peaks, turn your mixer off. If you're finding that the peaks are not stiff and the icing is still thin, turn your mixer back on, keep going, and have a little faith—it will get there. Royal icing can be a bit finicky the first few times you give it a whirl, but soon you'll be BFFs and you'll have it down!

Reminder: If you choose to use egg whites, find an alternative recipe. This recipe will NOT work with egg whites as a substitute.

Get the Right Color with the Right Products

There is a huge variety of food coloring out there. Although the majority of them will give you colorful happy results, for the purpose of royal icing, I would highly suggest using gel coloring. The four little squeeze bottles of color that were the center of any baking project when we were kids just won't cut it for your soon to be cookie masterpieces!

I typically stick to the brands ProGel and AmeriColor. ProGel colors come in a variety of really bright colors that are what I reach for first when I am mixing colors. There are also some AmeriColor hues that I can't live without; these are typically specialty colors such as gold and the darker hues. This book's recipes will make use of AmeriColor's "Bright White," "Chocolate Brown," "Gold," "Copper (Flesh Tone)," "Super Black," and "Super Red." AmeriColor is a nice option for beginners because they come in small 0.75oz bottles, which are perfect if you're looking to purchase a variety of colors without committing to large quantities.

If I do not specify the brand, you can assume that I am referencing a ProGel color. Note that I am not sponsored by either company, I truly just love their products—so ProGel, if you see this, call me!

Mixing Colors & Filling Piping Bags

Have you met the color wheel? I would suggest you find yourself a picture of it and get comfortable with it. I have to admit I do not know a lot about color theory, but the basics have become my best friend and my biggest asset when working on mixing colors. This is especially important if you don't plan on purchasing more than the primary colors in food colorings. Knowing the color wheel will help you achieve different shades, match existing colors, and find the best complementary colors.

This is a time-consuming process! I would recommend making a list of all the colors you plan on using for a particular batch and mixing them all at once. That way, when you are ready to sit down to decorate, you can really focus on what is in front of you.

Plan on mixing all your related colors in the same bowl. For example, I would mix all my pinks, reds, and oranges in the same bowl. Not only does this save on the number of dishes, it gives your colors a more cohesive look overall. Always start with your lightest colors and work in order all the way to your darkest shade. These basic principles will apply when mixing any colors.

Single-serving dining bowls are the perfect size to mix colors in. Fill the bowl with royal icing to the top, leaving enough room to comfortably stir. Time to add your color! Remember, you can always add more color, but you can't take it away, so start with a very small amount; we're talking pin-sized amounts. Stir until completely combined, making sure there are no streaks of color, then add additional color until your desired shade is achieved. Small spatulas work best for this, but use what you have in the kitchen. Don't be afraid to mix different colors—this is where your color wheel will come in handy!

Fill Your Piping Bag

INGREDIENTS

- Tipless piping bag
- Royal Icing
- Rubber bands (optional)
- Spatula

DIRECTIONS

1. Take a cup and insert your tipless piping bag into the cup, folding the edges of the bag over the top. This allows you to have two free hands to fill your bag.
2. Add about one-third of the icing in the bowl to the piping bag.
3. Pick the piping bag up out of the cup, squeeze the icing to the bottom of the bag, and tie it off. Rubber bands can be used if the bag is too full or if you have trouble tying.

Flooding consistency is going to take the most practice out of any skill in this book. Be patient, and don't be afraid to ditch anything that isn't working and start over. Flooding icing is a thinned-out version of your piping consistency designed to self-level and create those smoothly iced cookies you've been drooling over.

Let's go! You have a bowl with two-thirds of the icing left in it ready for you.

4. Turn on your faucet to a very slow dribble. You are striving to achieve the texture of soap or honey. Take a moment to flip your bottle of honey upside down for reference. Just like with color, you can always add more water, so start with a very small amount!
5. Keep adding water and mixing until the icing smoothly falls off your spatula and slowly settles by itself. The icing should still be thick, and the process of self-leveling shouldn't be immediate.

Flooding icing consistency is one of the hardest elements to master. Royal icing should be dripping off your spatula and slowly settling out to form a smooth surface in the bowl. If the settling is happening immediately, the icing is too thin. This takes practice, and eventually you will learn the natural feel for flooding consistency.

Troubleshooting your flooding icing: If your icing is too thick and will not settle, remix with a little more water. Flooding icing that is too thick has an easy solution, but there really isn't much you can do for icing that is too thin besides starting over. Don't get discouraged when you have to throw the icing away. It will all be worth it when you have perfect cookies and don't have to fight the wrong consistency during the entire icing process.

6. Once you have that texture nailed, transfer your icing into your piping bag while it is in your cup. Icing will naturally settle in the tip, so all you need to do is tie off the bag.

Repeat with all your colors! The process is tedious and can take a large amount of time. During the holidays, I spend almost an entire day just mixing and bagging all the colors! It will be worth it when you get to sit with your cookies in front of you and all your colors are ready to go, so be patient!

If your piping icing is so thick it is hard to mix colors, add a few drops of water to soften it up. Icing that is too thick puts extra stress on your hand when squeezing the bags and can cause unnecessary breaking in your piping lines.

To free up your hands to fill a piping bag, use a cup or glass. By placing the bag in the cup and folding the excess over the edge, it creates a large opening to pour the icing into.

Tipless Bags vs. Tips

Welcome to the debate. There is no right or wrong answer here, both have their own pros and cons. I learned to decorate with tips and slowly transitioned to tipless bags over time using only specialty tips (some of which are featured in later chapters). Here is my take on each of them.

Tips

Using tips is really helpful when you're a beginner. It gives you consistent piping lines and even amounts of flooding icing coming out. You don't have to worry about cutting the correct hole size, and you can freely change the tips if you're using a coupler (no shame in looking up the definition). If you're willing to purchase tips, I would recommend a full set so you have a variety of specialty tips that are fun to play with. When using tips, I prefer using a size 2 to pipe and a size 10 for all your flooding; you may develop a different preference, but it is a good place to start. The amount of added washing was really what drove me to transition away from them.

Tipless

Moving on to tipless bags, which is what you will see featured in all the photos, they are bags specially designed to be used without tips by snipping off the ends to create your desired thickness. I love them so much I designed my own; they are super thin and disprove any of those rumors you might have heard about tipless bags! It can be frustrating when you cut the wrong size hole and have to re-bag the icing, but to me, it's worth the disposal aspect of the bags. I can't stress enough that this is all personal preference. You can create equally beautiful cookies with and without tips! Some of my baking idols use tips, but you do you!

Notes

- All your colors are mixed, now what? Any leftover royal icing in your mixing bowl should be transferred to an airtight container; it will stay fresh at room temperature for about two weeks. Icing separation is totally natural and unavoidable, so make sure to give the royal icing a good stir before using again. You may notice separation within your piping bags as early as an hour after preparing. Massage the bags until the icing in each bag is one uniform color before you decorate.

Chapter 3

Decorating Basics

We're here to decorate! Your cookies are baked, your colors are mixed, and by this time your patience is wearing thin—but you've made it! Let's learn how to decorate. We're going to dive into all the basics. Really master this chapter before moving on to the next chapters, which full of fun designs. Add a bookmark, because you will be referring back to this chapter often!

All those colors you worked so hard to mix? Let's put them to work!

- Snip a small hole in the tip of your tipless piping consistency bags. Give them a test on a flat paper towel for easy cleanup. You are trying to achieve about the thickness of a permanent marker line.
- Snip off more of the bag if the hole is too small. If the hole is too big, transfer the icing into a new bag and try again! The flood consistency bags should be snipped to a width about twice the size of the holes for the piping consistency bags.

- Once you get a sense of how large the hole should be, you'll be doing this in your sleep, because you repeat this process on every. Single. Bag!

Before you dive right into those cookies you spent all that time baking, let's get some practice on some paper. I know, I know—BORING—but this is a great place to get some practice in without wasting your cookies. Can I suggest making a copy of the template to practice on? Place the template on a cookie sheet and cover it with plastic wrap; this allows you to throw away the plastic wrap when completed and start again fresh without printing out a million copies.

Templates are up! Practice, practice, practice. The most important thing I can walk you through is how to lead your icing through lines, swirls, and any other obstacle that comes your way.

- To start the piping line, you want the tip of your piping bag to lightly make contact with the surface. Applying a steady medium pressure to your bag, lift your piping bag up about an inch and begin to lead the icing to where you want it to go. This creates smooth, straight lines.

◦ When you want to complete the segment, slowly make contact with the surface again and release the pressure on the bag.

You want to visualize getting your line from point A to point B—thinking ahead will make leading your icing more natural. GO SLOWLY! Speed is gained through lots of practice, just like any other skill! If your icing line should break before you are done, pick up right where you left off and keep going. This could be caused by an air pocket in your icing bag or simply by going too quickly; it's a common thing, so learn to work with it. You might notice some mistakes, especially anywhere you had your line break and you had to start again. On a cookie, flood icing will cover any mistakes, so don't fret in the beginning. Practice on the worksheet at least five times before you dive into your cookies. Feel free to create your own practice sheet, and don't be afraid to add text for added practice. When training my first employees to decorate,

I sent them home with new worksheets to practice every night; now, you can't tell which one of us decorated the cookies! I will tell you with sympathy that circles are the hardest shape to decorate. This is due to the fact that there is always one part of the circle that you will not see no matter which way you go. You'll either learn to work with it or just avoid circles like I do.

Now that you're a pro, let's set the cookie scene up for success. It is best to decorate your cookies right on the **cookie sheet**; this lowers the chance of any smudges or of you dropping (yes, dropping!) your cookies greatly. I prefer to rearrange the cookies so they are along the edges of the cookie sheet, preventing any unnecessary reaching later on. Leave the parchment paper under the cookies; soon it will be looking rather colorful from all the icing smudges. Your tray is ready to go!

Cookie tray, check! Icing bags, check! Ready for the most important tool EVER?! *Your needle tool.* Okay, I know you need a million tools, but you know what? Pick up some toothpicks or a kabob stick, and BAM: there you have your own needle tool! You'll be using these to fix any errors, pop any bubbles, and just smooth out the icing in general. Keep 'em handy! I typically keep mine on paper towels or a napkin—trust me, you'll use them.

One final tip: do you notice any uneven edges on your cookies? This is typically caused by butter bleed or just cookies spreading in the baking process a little too much for your liking. Use a **zester** to shave down any spots that are not up to par! Voilà, you will have the sharpest squares a baker could ask for! This is a totally optional step. Some recipes have no spread, and some have a lot, but it's all about what YOU like! My cookies spread, and sometimes it's okay, but other times I'm really searching for that sharp edge. Just keep this tip in your back pocket as an option for later down the road. You can shave your cookies' edges after the icing is completely dry as well; it can be the perfecting final step before packaging!

Are you ready? You have your tray of cookies, bags of icing colors with openings cut, a needle tool of any variety, and a few paper towels. Let's do this. Standing or sitting is a personal preference; I am happy to do either, but keeping the cookies at about waist level will be helpful. If you prefer a sitting position, make sure both feet are planted on the floor. I'm not trying to tell you how to live your life, but you will learn to appreciate a sturdy position.

Set the scene before you start to decorate. Make sure all your supplies are within arm's reach so you can focus all your attention on the cookies once you start.

The time has come. You pick your starting cookie and grab your piping bag, working through from point A to point B to completely outline the shape with your icing line. As a beginner, immediately pick up your flooding consistency bag, filling in the closed shape by following your outline and working your way to the center. Remember your icing is self-leveling, so you don't need to be precise; however, staying with the basic idea of following the outline and working your way to the center will help you achieve the perfect amount of icing. Too much icing will fall over the dam that your outline has created, and too little will not create a smooth cookie. This is where you might notice some bubbles in your icing or tiny gaps where your icing needs a little nudge to help as it self-levels; use your needle tool to help fix any blemishes. Repeat this with each of your cookies.

Leading your piped line helps create smooth, straight lines. Once you've made contact and started a line, you want to lead the icing and guide it along the edge of the cookie. Note how far away the tip of the bag is from the cookie. When your line is complete, slowly lower the piping back down to the cookie and release your pressure on the piping bag.

This part is really soothing and truly the part that can be addictive. As you gain speed with practice, I would suggest outlining an entire row of cookies and then coming back and flooding the entire row. You will have the cleanest looking edges when the outline is still wet; when you add the flood icing, it will form one clean edge. If you wait too long and the outline dries before you flood, you will see a distinct outline, which is why in the beginning, I suggest working on one cookie at a time. The best thing about working with cookies as your creative medium is that you can eat any evidence of a mistake. Literally. The other option is to scrape off any icing and start again; no one will ever know!

When flooding cookies, I always recommending tracing the outside piped line as a guide and working your way in until the entire cookie is covered. This helps ensure the correct amount of icing for those perfectly smooth puffy iced cookies.

Your iced cookie base is complete! Before moving on to additional decoration, let the cookies start to set for about 30 minutes before you add anything on top. This allows a top crust to form which will hold up any detail on top instead of melting right into your flood icing. Just like your outline, I would suggest completing all your decorating before your base is completely dry. This will help your detail bind to the base and help prevent any chipping or breakage when you're delivering them. As a rule of thumb, your cookies will need to dry overnight or for about 8 hours. This varies depending on your climate, so I would suggest having a few test cookies your first time. This is the only time your cookies will not be stored in an airtight container.

Using your needle
tool, toothpick, or
whatever sharp item you've
deemed appropriate for the
job, fix any blemishes such as
air bubbles or uneven icing.
Make sure the icing is still
wet to avoid making any
problems worse.

Like I said before, get very comfortable with this chapter. Don't be afraid to stop here. Simple chubby hearts decorated with one color are still pretty cute! Remember we all have to start somewhere. There was no book to help me when I started, so you're already ahead of me! Good luck!

Notes

- A zester or a fine grater works best to shave down any edges. You can see the one photographed; it was made with the intention of zesting a lemon and can be found at any cooking store.

- Observe how I am holding the piping bags. I find I have the most control over my piping bag when I am gripping and squeezing from the top of the bag with one hand and lightly touching my other (non-dominant) hand to the bag for an extra boost of steadiness. Using large piping bags filled to the top can cause hand cramps for me, so I prefer to make several bags filled three-fourths of the way full for comfort.

- Piping bags that are not in use but already cut open may spill some icing out. Use a cool and clean cookie sheet to hold them, resting the tips at a slight bend against the edges to prevent any leaking. Icing left in the tips may crust over; gently break up and remove before piping.

Chapter 4

A Basket Full of Spring

By now, you've mastered cookie basics and you're ready to create something fun and exciting! Spring is a bright fresh start to the year, so let's dive into a new skill that can be applied to many designs no matter what season it is!

Follow instructions in Chapter 1 to cut and bake Easter basket cookies. The same design principles can be applied to any basket-*ish* cutter. Prepare a batch of royal icing while your cookies are cooling. In this chapter, you will need both pipe and flood icings in white and warm brown. Adding "Bright White" AmeriColor coloring to all of your white icing will counteract any dullness that the vanilla may have brought to the color, ensuring that your cookies' color will pop! Warm brown is best achieved using AmeriColor "Chocolate Brown" by adding 1-2 drops to a small bowl of white royal icing. You will need a grass green in pipe consistency icing only, which can be created with a few drops of "leaf green" ProGel. During this time of year, I really embrace the pastel shades, which can be achieved by using smaller amounts of coloring.

Refer to the "wet on wet" technique in Chapter 10 to help you create these simple but sweet Easter eggs on your own.

Easter Basket Cookies

INGREDIENTS

- Basket-shaped cookies
- Brown icing, both pipe and flood consistencies

DIRECTIONS

1. Starting with the base of the basket only, use your brown pipe consistency icing to outline the shape of your base, closing off the dam by piping a straight line across the cookie at the top of the widest section.
2. Fill the basket in with brown flood icing and set aside to allow the icing to set.
3. Trace the top edge of the cookie with your brown pipe consistency icing again, then follow the same line about ¼ inch toward the center of the cookie to create the handle with the same warm brown.

4. Flood the thin curved line. The only exposed part of the cookie left should be a semi-circle that should next be carefully flooded with white. Set cookies aside.

To practice a basket-weave pattern on the parchment before taking it to the cookies:

1. Start with all the vertical lines working from the center line outwards. An odd number of lines looks the most realistic.
2. Making short horizontal lines that cross one vertical line at a time, cross every other vertical line. Begin the second row of horizontal lines in the alternate vertical lines, i.e., the ones you didn't cross in the first row of horizontal lines.
3. Repeating this process working down the vertical lines will create a basket-weave pattern.

This pattern will help you learn control of the piping bag and the repetitive process of the tiny lines. Once you are satisfied with how your basket weave looks on paper, apply the same exact principles to the basket base of the cookie.

•

Drumroll please...this section's lesson is how to create realistic leaves using a tipless bag! For those of you who decided to purchase a set of tips, there are several different options you can use, so give those a whirl. This lesson is for the tipless bag diehards like myself.

When using a piping bag with a cut leaf tip, always make sure the seam is pointed toward the ceiling for healthy leaves every time.

To Make a Leaf Tip with a Tipless Bag

INGREDIENTS

- Green leaf icing, pipe consistency only
- Piping bag

DIRECTIONS

1. Take your leaf green piping consistency bag you made previously in your hand.
2. Pinch any icing that is in the tip up into the bag a short way, so nothing spills out.
3. Flatten the tip of the icing bag along the seam.
4. Cut the tip off the bag to create your standard sized piping hole.

5. In the center of the hole on the flattened bag, cut a vertical slit about ¼ inch long. (To create larger leaves, cut a larger opening with a proportionally sized vertical slit.)

To create larger leaves, cut a larger hole opening with a proportionally sized vertical slit.

Now, for the piping:

1. When you go to pipe your leaves, rotate the bag so the seam of the bag is pointing toward the ceiling.
2. Squeezing your piping bag while you make contact with the cookie, slowly pull back; release pressure on the bag when the desired size of leaf has been achieved. A way to create another variety of leaf is after you've made contact and are slowly pulling back, pulse the pressure you're using for a more exaggerated look.

Just like any other skill, don't be afraid to practice on paper before you graduate to the cookies. Leaves have a messy look to begin with, so embrace it! Leaves are going to be one of your most commonly used skills, so really take the time to figure it out. They're not limited to spring, since they're also found on bridal cookies, pumpkins in the fall, and holly in the winter months, you can't escape it!

Now that you've mastered the leaf tip, add two rows of leaves at the top of the basket to create Easter grass. I add a fun spring sprinkle on the grass for festive detail, but this is totally optional. This is also a great way to hide any errors you've made with the leaves. Let cookies dry completely before storing in an airtight container.

P.S.: Remember when I said plain decorated cookies are still equally gorgeous? Pipe and flood some solid colored eggs, and utilize your sprinkle mix (see note below) by adding them to the bottom half of the eggs before they dry. You'll have a gorgeous spread of happy cookies to share!

Notes

- Purchase an Easter themed sprinkle mix full of bunnies and eggs for added detail. The next chapter will walk you through how to make your own sprinkle mix at no additional cost.

Chapter 5

I Scream, You Scream... for Summer!

Everyone seems to be consuming all the ice cream in the summer, and we don't blame them! It's the perfect treat when you're trying to cool off on a hot day and satisfy that sweet tooth. You can't scroll through social media without seeing dozens of cones featuring the perfect "drip" of ice cream. Here is my take on a cool classic that is guaranteed to be a hit on your social media with endless likes—and bonus, no brain freezes!

Homemade Sprinkles

This is the time to pick your favorite summer colors! These will be used in your homemade sprinkles mix. As you can see, I chose to do a playful summer pink mix. This mix included two shades of pink and two shades of tangerine, with a sky blue to pop. Have fun with this! Play off a theme or your favorite colors. This is a great opportunity to utilize any leftover icing colors you might have on hand from another design. You will only need piping consistencies for the colors used to make sprinkles.

INGREDIENTS

- Icing in desired colors, piping consistency only
- Cookie sheet
- Parchment paper
- Needle tool
- Sharp knife
- Airtight container, for storage

DIRECTIONS

1. Line a cookie sheet with parchment paper, making sure the paper is cut to the right size and lies flat on the cookie sheet.
2. Pipe straight lines across the cookie sheet; this can be done quickly and doesn't need to be perfect—no need to fix any broken piping lines.
3. Fill up the cookie sheet with a variety of colorful lines.
4. Set aside to dry for about an hour.
5. Check on your sprinkles. Lines should be completely dry.
6. At this time, either use a sharp knife to cut the lines into tiny bits or crumble the lines with your hands.
7. Mix up the colors and store in an airtight container.

For a fun and easy nod to the 4th of July, make a batch of red, white, and blue sprinkles. Top your cookies, cakes, and real melting ice cream cones with them. Don't limit your sprinkle usage to just the cookies, share the fun with all your sweets! At my 4th of July barbecue, you will find huge homemade marshmallow cereal bars with the sprinkles mixed right in.

Ice Cream Cone Cookies with Sprinkles

INGREDIENTS

- Ice cream cone-shaped cookies
- AmeriColor's "Chocolate Brown" color icing, pipe and flood consistencies
- AmeriColor's "Bright White" color icing, pipe and flood consistencies
- Homemade Sprinkles
- Royal Icing
- Airtight container, for storage

DIRECTIONS

1. Follow instructions in Chapter 1 to cut out and bake your ice cream cones. There is a huge variety of ice cream cone cutter shapes and sizes. I encourage you to mix and match cutters to create the perfect variety for your cookies.
2. Prepare a batch of royal icing. While the cookies are cooling, take the time to mix your colors. For the ice cream cones, you will need both pipe and flood icing consistencies in "Warm Brown" / "Bright White." Adding "Bright White" AmeriColor coloring to all of your white icing will counteract any dullness that the vanilla may have brought to the color. Warm brown is best achieved using AmeriColor's "Chocolate Brown" by adding 1 to 2 drops to a small bowl of white royal icing.
3. Now make your sprinkles if you haven't already.
4. While the soon to be sprinkles are hardening, it is time to start decorating the cones. Pick up your warm brown piping consistency bag.
5. Starting at the tip of the cone, follow the straight edges until the point where you reach the circular "ice cream scoop" part of the cookie; this is where

you will close the triangle. Using your flooding consistency icing, slowly fill in the triangle by tracing the piped line and working your way to the center.

6. Let icing self-level, then use your needle tool to pop bubbles and fix any blemishes.
7. Check on your sprinkles and continue to follow directions in Homemade Sprinkles recipe.
8. Now, let's add the ice cream. Using your white piping bag, outline the half circle that the top of the cone makes.
9. Fill in the piped area with white flooding consistency icing. At this point, there will be a small gap of cookie between the cone and half circle that is left naked. Ice cream naturally has texture, so any mistakes will look intentional, don't be afraid of them!
10. Let cookies sit about 30 minutes while the flooded icing sets slightly.
11. Add detail to the cones by creating a cross-hatch pattern with the brown icing. Start at the tip by making an "X" shape and work your way up the top of the cone repeating the "X" pattern.

For a bright seasonal summertime flavor, substitute lemon extract for vanilla extract in the royal icing. This is a fresh twist on classic sugar cookies.

12. Fill in the blank section of cookie with your white flooding consistency. Work in a tight loop pattern from left to right, covering a small portion of both the white ice cream and the brown cone. This messy detail creates a realistic texture.
13. Add the final touch with a pinch of your freshly made colorful sprinkles!
14. Let cookies dry in the open overnight, or for about 8 hours depending on your location and the summer heat. Make sure cookies are completely dry before storing in an airtight container.

Now you can show up to your next ice cream social with a batch of these and be the talk of the party!

•

Don't feel bogged down by plain vanilla ice cream, challenge yourself to recreate your frozen delights in cookie form. Add whipped cream, cherries, chocolate sauce—any topping is fair game! Try making my personal favorite flavor, mint chocolate chip with green icing and chocolate sprinkles.

I absolutely love making sprinkles because they are an easy way to add detail to your cookies without having to buy any additional supplies. Don't feel limited to using sprinkles in only realistic scenarios; some other great places to utilize them are on Christmas trees, to add flair to basic shapes, and on baby themed cookies for a whimsical touch.

Notes

- Make sprinkles mixes out of leftover colors, then store in an airtight container until the perfect occasion arises to utilize that color palette.

Chapter 6

Fall – Pumpkins

As a Midwest girl, I welcome fall with open arms! There is something about the feeling of the seasonal shift when the air turns crisp and the colors start to change. Hot summer nights turn into cool fall evenings. People gather for football games; hot beverages are passed around, and everything is magically pumpkin-flavored. In this chapter, I really want to do more with less, which is why I am demonstrating three different ways to decorate a pumpkin cookie to celebrate all the moments of fall. Trust me, you'll be wanting to wear your best fall flannel after this.

I am always in an imaginative head space trying to dream up new content, just like any person in a creative industry. I love sharing the process, from giving sneak peeks to the final reveal. Sometimes things aren't received as well as I hoped, but the best is when the simplest of concepts takes off. One of our most popular cookies ever happened to be the simplest ombré pumpkins you ever did see! I couldn't pass up the opportunity to add my favorite color—pink—into my fall color palette, and I encourage you to do the same to create an extra special personalized set by sticking to who you are.

Let's dive into how to make the only fall cookie you'll need, a pumpkin! The key to keeping these really simple but visually interesting is by adding dimension. This is a great skill to apply to all your cookies moving forward, so let's get right to it.

Pumpkin Cookies

INGREDIENTS

- Pumpkin-shaped cookies
- Airtight container, for storage
- Icing in 2–4 colors (recommended shades ProGel's "Pink" and "Tangerine"), both pipe and flood consistencies

DIRECTIONS

1. Follow instructions in Chapter 1 to cut out and bake your pumpkins. If you have a variety of shapes and sizes, feel free to bake a variety, this is an easy way to add visual detail.

For ombré pumpkins, you will need four different shades of color in pipe and flood consistencies. Notice I chose a subtle variety of orange to pink shades for the ombré effect. I used ProGel's "Pink" and "Tangerine" to achieve these colors. To create a traditional ombré effect, create four different shades of the same color, but don't shy away from stretching two colors over four shades. When mixing colors, start with the lightest color; mix all four colors in the same bowl, finishing with the darkest shade. This tip will help you with achieving the perfect saturation of each color to create an easy ombré.

2. Fill all eight piping bags with icing in flood and pipe consistencies. Warm brown in pipe and flood consistencies will also be used. Suggestion: mix the brown icing in the same bowl, as the little bit of color will create the perfect tone of brown for your cookies.

Picture a real pumpkin and how the texture creates these natural sections. We want to recreate this on our cookies. Start by outlining the edge of the pumpkin in your first color choice.

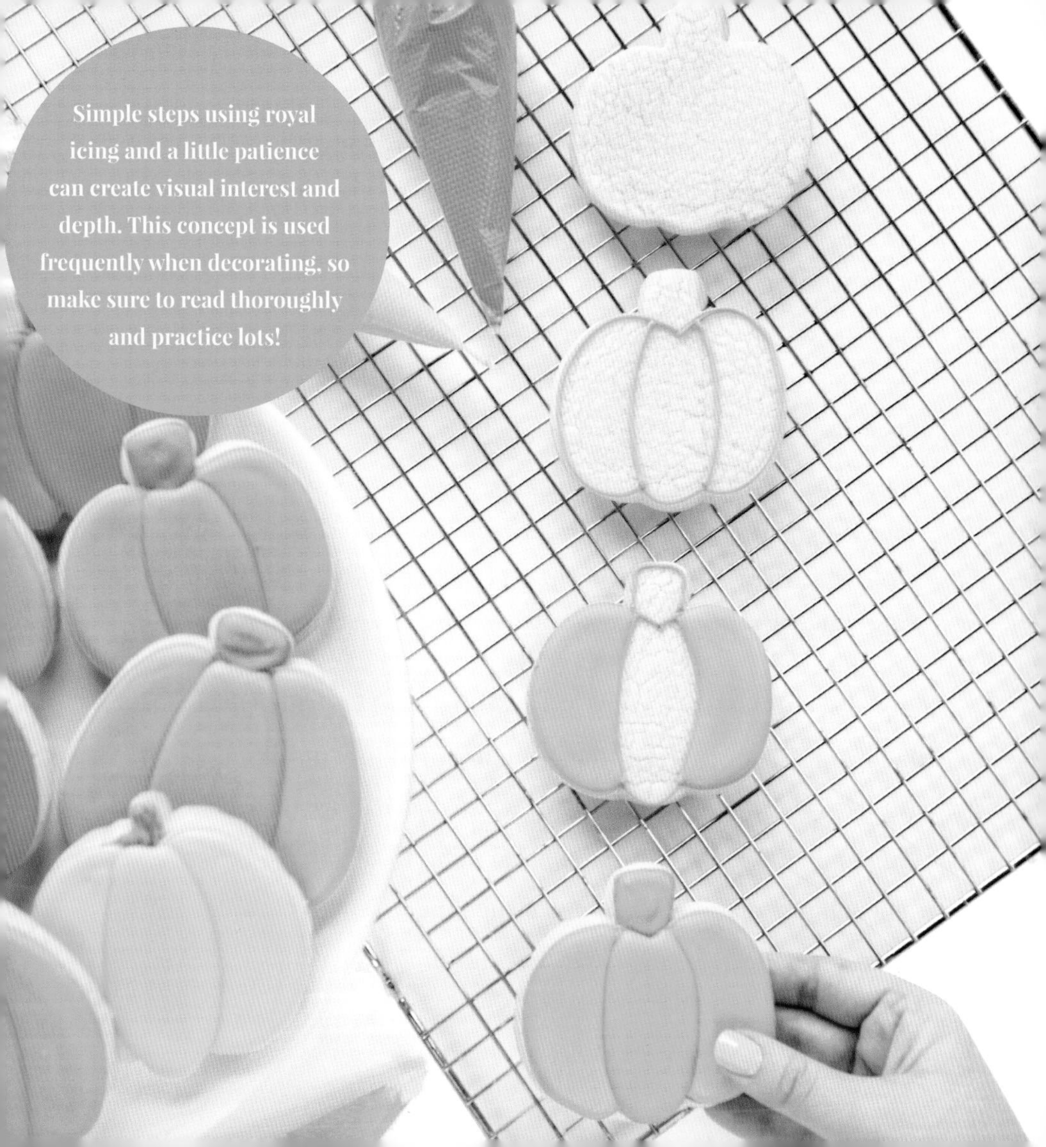
Simple steps using royal icing and a little patience can create visual interest and depth. This concept is used frequently when decorating, so make sure to read thoroughly and practice lots!

3. Next, using the bottom edges in the cookie as a guide, add your middle section with two additional lines, creating three sections total. Try to make the lines billow outwards for a more natural curve. Take your flooding icing in the same color and fill in the two outer sections.
4. Set pumpkins aside for about 30 minutes or until the flooding icing sets. Once the cookies have formed a solid top crust, it is time to go back and flood the center.
5. Follow the edges slowly and more precisely than typical flooding. Work your way to the center until completely full, adding just a hair more icing for an added puff but being cautious not to add so much the icing spills over. Repeat these steps in the warm brown to create the stem.

This is where your icing texture is key. You will not have that great puffy looking icing if your flooding icing is too thin; this is the hardest thing to master. Trial and error is the only way to learn. It can be frustrating but remember, I've been in your shoes! Refer to Chapter 2 for all your royal icing information if you keep struggling. If your flooding icing is too thin, it will not hold any shape, making it impossible to create depth.

6. Repeat all the steps with your different colors to create the ombré pumpkins. Let cookies dry overnight or until completely dry before storing in an airtight container.

Before we dive into the other two cookie designs, keep in mind that while these pumpkins are beautiful on their own, they can also be used as a canvas for all your creative seasonal ideas. By the end of this book, you will be able to come back to these pumpkins and utilize all kinds of techniques to jazz them up! You can add messages, a little metallic decoration for an elegant fall event, or ruffles for a fall due date. Later you will learn how to add a floral piece for a gorgeous Thanksgiving.

Jack-o'-Lantern Cookies

Boo! It's Halloween and we're carving jack-o'-lanterns!

INGREDIENTS

- Pumpkin-shaped cookies
- Orange and warm brown colored icing, both pipe and flood consistencies
- Black colored icing, pipe consistency only
- Airtight container, for storage

DIRECTIONS

1. Start with your blank canvas: perfectly baked pumpkin cookies. You will need both icing in both pipe and flood consistencies in orange and warm brown.

Pumpkins come in all different shapes, colors, and sizes so don't get too hung up on finding the perfect shade. My personal preference is to use ProGel "Orange" for a brighter orange during Halloween. You will also need black in pipe consistency only. Black can be a difficult color to achieve; I recommend using AmeriColor "Super Black." Add in small amounts until the dark shade is achieved. This is also a great place to utilize other colors that you are finished with by mixing them all together, which typically creates a swamp-like color. Do not fret, the black food coloring will mask any trace of anything other than black, and you will end up using less coloring. This is one of the best tips to reduce both waste and cost!

2. Swipe a thin layer of black icing across the cookie, making sure the black icing evenly covers the cookie.
3. Pick up your orange piping bag and outline the pumpkin's edge. Take creative liberty here and pipe your best jack-o'-lantern face! As you can see, I chose a toothy smile, but anything from goofy to scary will do the trick. One thing to note while creating your face is to make sure the center of your design is completely covered in black, as this creates a realistic jack-o'-lantern feel; no blank cookie should be showing.

Mini spatulas are one of my favorite tools when working with royal icing. They're the perfect size to mix colors, and in this case, to smear black icing across the cookie for the base of the jack-o'-lantern. You can typically find them seasonally, since they are the perfect size for stocking stuffers... hint, hint!

4. Slowly fill in the pumpkin with the orange flood consistency, leaving the center of the face design black.
5. Once the flood icing has started to set, repeat the pipe and flood process with warm brown on the stem.
6. Let cookies dry overnight or until completely dry before storing in an airtight container.

•

Halloween cookies are a great opportunity to branch out to new designs with your newly learned skills! White ghosts with simple faces and bright pieces of candy make for easy designs guaranteed to impress! Use the cookies in the photos to inspire you to get creative on your own!

Side note: Don't feel obligated to stick with just faces, you can make jack-o'-lanterns inspired by your favorite sports teams, logos, or even animals. Get inspired by popular trends—did I see striped pumpkins? Yes, please!

Thanksgiving Floral Cookies

Turkey Day! This seems to be the time of year for beautiful tablescapes and funny "gobble till you wobble" sayings! I want to help you achieve elevated designs for Thanksgiving while keeping the design and supplies simple! The best part is that this concept of a floral topper can be added to all your designs, plaques, celebration cakes, bridal cookies, or anything you want to have an extra added pop of elegance.

INGREDIENTS

- Fully decorated pumpkin-shaped cookies that have dried (refer to the Pumpkin Cookies in the beginning of this chapter for colors and adding depth)
- Icing in 4 floral colors, piping consistency only
- Leaf green icing, in piping consistency only, with a leaf slit cut into the tip (refer to Chapter 4 for questions on piping leaves)
- White pearl sprinkles (to create the exact florals in the image)
- A number 18 metal tip
- Airtight container, for storage

What colors to use for florals are a personal choice. As you can see, I used a variety of colors that complement each other, but a monochromatic color scheme is also a fan favorite! Also, I'm using a tip with tipless bags here—ironic, right? But trust me, they're quick and easy when you're adding little details to cookies.

Using the same leaf tip technique you learned in Chapter 4, you'll be able to add an elegant floral piece to your pumpkins.

DIRECTIONS

1. Starting with an empty bag, hold up the tip to the pointed end of the bag and cut the opening of the bag halfway up the tip. This creates an opening that is the perfect size for the next step, which is opening the bag and inserting the tip.
2. Now place the bag with the tip already inserted in a cup; fold the sides over the lip of the cup and fill with your favorite floral piping color. Tie up the bag and give the icing a squeeze until the icing emerges from the tip. This first flower will be the largest and the center of attention, so pick your favorite spot for its placement.
3. Hold your piping bag perpendicular to the cookie, start at the center of the flower, and moving in a counterclockwise motion, create a swirl; either go around twice or stop at your preferred size.
4. Moving on to your next flower, use a different color to pipe a large dot next to your large center flower. Immediately add 3 pearl sprinkles; push them down into the icing to create the floral center.

5. Flower number three will be your second largest flower. Pipe a dot that is only slightly smaller than your center flower.
6. Using the same color and starting from the outside edge, outline the dot and create a swirl ending in the center.
7. The final flower type is really simple, and it is designed to fill in any "holes" in the design you think are visually missing something. You will find odd numbers look best; I chose to create three flowers. Pipe small dots in your last floral color, and quickly add a single pearl sprinkle to the center, pushing it in for added detail.
8. The final touch is adding leaves. Make sure your green piping bag has a leaf slit. A good rule of thumb is smaller flowers need one leaf, while bigger florals need 2–3.
9. Play around with what you like; this is the last step, and your final touches should add a cohesive polished look to the floral piece. Since the your cookies that you are using for a base are already dry, you will only need 1–2 hours for the floral detail to set completely before you're able to store them in an airtight container.

This chapter was a big one, covering three different designs and two holidays, all with one cutter. I hope your new skills will encourage you to branch out and trust your own creative eye and to explore your own designs. Small changes to the same cookies can have such a large impact.

Notes

- For those of you looking to skip a few steps (hello, me!), using all white flowers gives an added touch of elegance to your pumpkins without having to make any additional colors.
- Pumpkins naturally grow on vines; add this detail onto your cookies using brown or green piping for a more realistic vibe.

Chapter 7

Winter Theme

The holidays are over and the days are short. What better way to pass the time than baking? Hunker down on your next snow day and learn a new skill. Grab some hot cocoa because we are making snowflakes and mittens this chapter. We are focusing on adding texture and visual interest to your cookies.

Snowflake Cookies

INGREDIENTS

- Snowflake-shaped cookies
- "Bright White" colored icing, pipe and flood consistencies
- Homemade Sprinkles
- Sanding sugar
- Airtight container, for storage

DIRECTIONS

1. Per the instructions in Chapter 1, cut and bake snowflake cookies. If a variety of shapes and sizes are available, I encourage you to cut out a large variety. No two snowflakes are the same, so challenge yourself to make all your snowflake cookies unique!

For the icing, you will be using both pipe and flood consistencies in Bright White. Decide on your own what color palette you would like to use to add the details. White on white adds a really glamorous element, while bright colors give a more whimsical feel. I tend to grab whatever colors I am already using in the kitchen that day, which as I'm sure you can guess usually include a lot of pink! For the snowflakes in the images, I used ProGel "Pink" and "Ice Blue" and AmeriColor "Royal Blue." Again, using the same bowl to mix all of your colors will give them a polished, cohesive look.

2. Pipe and flood all the snowflake bases in "Bright White". Take your time piping the edges; there are a lot of small details and crevices to follow, but after a few times around you will find your rhythm.
3. Flood your cookies and then let the bases of the cookies dry completely. This is important, because we are adding going to be adding sprinkles to the piped detail on top. If the base is not dry, the sprinkles will stick to the base and you'll be left with sprinkle-covered blobs. Trust me, be patient here!
4. Once your bases are dry, add the colorful snowflake patterns. I like to start by connecting each apex to the apex on the opposite side. Refer to the photos: I piped three straight lines to connect all six apexes. This is not a hard and fast rule to follow, but it's a great place to start when you're a little hesitant.

I like to add a mixture of dots and small lines; some snowflakes have a more angular look, while others are softer with dots and rounds.

5. As soon as your snowflake design is complete, immediately sprinkle the cookie with clear sanding sugar. The clear sugar allows the color of the icing to pop while adding the icy glistening appearance of the sprinkles.

There is a difference between granulated sugar and sanding sugar, so please do not use them interchangeably. The use of traditional everyday baking sugar will leave your cookies looking dull and dusty. Sanding sugar is cheap and easy to obtain; you should be able to pick some up at your local grocery. Yes, it's that easy!

6. Cover the cookies completely with the sprinkles and let the icing set for a few minutes.
7. Pick up each cookie and shake off any extra sprinkles back into the container. Repeat until all your snowflakes are uniquely decorated.
8. Let dry completely; at this stage, only the added detail should be wet. The cookies will then be ready to store in an airtight container.

No two snowflakes are the same, take on the challenge of mixing up your cookie designs as well! It's fun to use a variety of colors and designs.

Are you a mittens or gloves person? This is a serious debate in my house. For the sake of decorating cute mittens instead of gloves that end up looking like creepy colored hands, today you will be a mittens-only guy or gal!

INGREDIENTS

- Mitten-shaped cookies
- Airtight container, for storage
- White, pink, light blue, and royal blue colored icing, both pipe and flood consistencies

DIRECTIONS

1. Cut and bake your mittens from the instructions in Chapter 1. I love to coordinate the colors of the snowflakes to the mittens, so to do that, you will need pipe and flood consistencies in the colors mentioned above.

2. Pipe and flood the hand of your cookie, leaving the bottom wrist section uncovered for now. When piping, really emphasize the indent between the fingers and the thumb.
3. Set aside to let the flood icing set for about 30 minutes.
4. In the meantime, let's practice the weave of the mittens so they appear to be knitted. Refer to the weave patterns we practiced in Chapter 3; we want to recreate the same motion only vertical this time. Practice on the parchment paper first. Pipe five vertical waves. Working left to right, immediately return to your first wave. At the same starting point, create a second vertical wave in the opposite direction, overlapping at the center line. This creates your basic weave pattern that will be applied to the mittens.
5. Now that your mittens are set, starting at the indent between the thumb and the mitt, create a vertical *line* to the base of the flooded color. Working your way to the left, add vertical lines with small gaps between each one.

For beginners, I would recommend larger gaps to give you plenty of space to create your weave pattern. The closer together the lines are, the more precise your piping needs to be. The overall aesthetic will be the same, it is just a matter of how tight the knitting on your mittens will appear.

6. On the thumb, to the right of the first vertical line, add lines at a 45-degree angle that butt up right to the vertical line. This adds the realistic visual interest of a true knitted mitten.
7. Immediately start adding in the weave pattern you've been practicing. I prefer to add the knit design to every other gap, especially when you're cranking out hundreds of these—your hand will thank you! But for your gorgeous dozen that you're working on at home, feel free to add the knit design into every gap with the weave pattern.
8. Once all the detail is complete, pipe and flood the wrist of the mitten in an alternate color; as you can see, I chose white to keep all the different colored mittens cohesive.
9. Let the cookies dry completely for about eight hours before storing in an airtight container.

The beauty of these cookies is that you can utilize them all season long. They're not just for curing those post-holiday blues. We create countless batches of these during the month of December for people who want to wish others happy holidays without getting holiday specific.

•

Both of these techniques can be utilized in other areas. There are plenty of ways to add texture to your cookies, but I tend to reach for these first. When using sprinkles, I prefer to use house made royal icing sprinkles or sanding sugar. Sprinkles can add textural variety and even flavor to your cookies. There are tons of gorgeous mixes out there and plenty that I utilize myself. However, when shopping, be aware that candy, chocolate, and sometimes other add-on items may be included that are simply decorative and not actually edible. Buyer beware!

The basket weave from the Easter baskets and the weave used to create a knitting appearance are the first of countless patterns you will utilize throughout your cookie decorating experience. I hope you become inspired by how realistic and easy recreating patterns can be. Other pattern suggestions include roping and plaids. Get inspired! They are some of the most tedious details to do, but they really make an impact, so it is worth the extra time. I think you just found your next snow day activity.

Notes

- Colored sanding sugar will absolutely work in this scenario. I would suggest coordinating the color of the sprinkles with the icing for more of a finished look. Investing in a bottle of clear sanding sugar is perfect because it appears to be the color that is underneath it while still giving a sparkling effect. Bonus, you are only storing one jar in your pantry!

Chapter 8

Bridal

Welcome to the shiniest chapter yet. We're talking all things bridal, and that means BLING! Engagement rings are by far our most requested cookies. They're a festive and fun addition to one of the most celebrated events in life. You'll see I mixed them with some chubby hearts, for which I'll talk about the most polarizing, or should I say aggravating, topic: adding text! You'll be adding "Mrs." on all the hearts before you know it as well as making stacks of conversation hearts to celebrate your best gals in February.

For this chapter, you'll need edible gold dust. When shopping around for this, read the label and make sure it states that it is "edible." It's expensive but cherished; I'm making it sound like it should be stored in my jewelry box. You will also need the highest percentage of grain alcohol your state allows; we'll touch on the reasoning behind this later. Now we're talking, here comes the party! And no, it is not for drinking if your cookies don't turn out.

Engagement Ring Cookies

INGREDIENTS

- Engagement ring-shaped cookies
- Round metal cutter
- Royal icing
- White and gold icing, both pipe and flood consistencies
- Gold dust (edible)
- High proof alcohol
- Paintbrush (food grade)
- Airtight container, for storage

DIRECTIONS

1. Follow the instructions in Chapter 1 to cut and bake your engagement ring cookies. While the cookies are still warm on the tray, take a small round metal cutter (make sure it is metal, plastic cutters may melt!) and cut out

the center of the ring. I prefer to do this after they have baked because it gives you a crisp, round center. If you prefer to do this before baking, that is perfectly fine; if you decide after the cookies are baked that the look isn't up to your standards, use the small round cutter to cut off anything extra for a sharp, perfect center circle.

2. Leave the cookies to finish cooling. You can either dispose of the round centers, or to be honest, I would keep them as a snack for while you're decorating.
3. Make a batch of royal icing; for the rings you will need both pipe and flood consistencies in white and gold. Gold is one of the specialty colors I referred to in Chapter 2 that is made by AmeriColor. About 3-4 drops of coloring per bowl will do the trick. There is no perfect shade of gold because it will be painted over later, it simply provides a solid base (or a primer, for you HGTV fans).
4. With your gold pipe consistency (that to be honest, looks more like buttercup), pipe the outline of the band. Ugh, circles! Make sure to include the prongs, leaving a sharp point for the diamond. Flood the gold outline and set the cookie aside to set.

Paint cookies with a thin even coating; any streaks or globs may cause a dusty gold mess later on. Adding a metallic to any cookie design will elevate the design. See those chubby pink hearts? Give a large brush stroke of gold one side for a glamorous touch.

For food safety, make sure you purchase food grade paint brushes, which you can find at most local craft stores. The extra step of hand-painting the gold onto the dry cookie is worth every second—it's such an eye-catching touch!

5. With your white piping, close the diamond by adding the top 3 sides. You do not need to pipe white against the prongs on the bottom of the diamond, because the flooded gold will act as your dam in this case and because of the dimensional principle from Chapter 6. This principle applies anytime you are flooding two colors next to each other. Make sure the first color is set beforehand to avoid any bleeding or blurred lines.
6. Did you double-check to see if the gold is set? Flood your diamond! Set your cookies aside. Cookies should be completely dry before you add the gold, otherwise, if you try to paint gold any sooner, you will have a sticky mess on your hands. This will take anywhere from 6 to 8 hours depending on your location.

Time to pull out your gold dust and high percentage alcohol. If you cannot use alcohol for reasons such as age or beliefs, water will work, but it won't have the same super shiny results. If you're just trying to use up leftover cheap alcohol from the other weekend, don't. One of the most common questions I receive is about how I get my cookies to shine so well, and the secret is in the alcohol. If you're curious to test my theory, feel free to raid your bar cart and stage a very scientific experiment on your own time. The higher the percentage, the quicker the evaporation is, which leaves your cookies extra shiny.

7. Mix the alcohol and gold dust to create a paint-like texture. I would suggest using an eye dropper to add small amounts of alcohol at a time, stirring with your paint brush. There are food grade paint brushes, please invest in them instead of raiding the craft box. The dust can be reused after the alcohol evaporates, so it is best to mix them in a container that you can seal up for storage in order to use the dust in the future. Paint palettes are also a great option as shown in the photos; this is perfect for small amounts of gold paint.
8. Paint the dry gold surface with your freshly mixed gold paint. Aim for an even layer, avoiding any thick spots that may cause smearing later. This process can be tedious, especially working with small areas and text, but the results are so worth it!

During the painting process, keep an eye on the thickness of the paint; the alcohol evaporates, and additional drops added throughout the painting process are the key to success. Before you ask about cookies for your BFF and her brand-new platinum engagement ring, yes, these same principles apply to any metallic dust (just make sure you get the edible kind!).

The last step is piping the white details onto the diamond. I know I went against what I said earlier about it being best to pipe and flood everything while it is still wet, but hear me out. Piping only details will dry quickly in comparison to flood icing, and just in case you went rogue with that paint brush and smeared a bit onto the diamond, the detail will cover it right up.

9. Outline the diamond and add the final geometric details as seen in the photos. Cookies will be completely dry in about 30 minutes. Minor smearing with the gold is normal.

As you can see in the photos, I decided to pair these with bride and groom cookies and chubby hearts! Hey, it's just me, proving my point from Chapter 3 that simple flooded cookies are still gorgeous, especially mixed in with other designs. If you're not sold on the blank hearts, they are the perfect place to add text! The wedding date, "Mrs.," the wedding location—the possibilities are endless.

We didn't cover step-by-step instructions to decorating the wedding dress and tuxedo. By now, however, you have all the skills to take on this challenge yourself. Tip: you can repurpose most gift box cutter shapes into a tuxedo; if you're looking for more of a casual look, ditch the jacket and add suspenders.

Strategically place
cookies and other sweets
around the party for an added
sugar bonus, not to mention
an adorable theme display!
Check out Chapter 12 for other
fun ideas for displaying
cookies.

Although text isn't necessary to create gorgeous cookies that get the point across, the added personalization makes it fun. This can also be a really sticky part of decorating cookies, so I just wanted to dip into the basics without going into crazy fonts, logos, or longer sayings. I took the hearts from the bridal set and added some simple text to create conversation hearts in a nod to Valentine's Day.

Throw in come conversation heart candies, some champagne, and a few disco balls and you're ready for the best Valentine's your friends could ask for.

Valentine's Day Cookies

INGREDIENTS

- Heart-shaped cookies
- Icing in "Pink" ProGel in pipe and flood consistency
- Icing in "Super Red" AmeriColor, pipe and flood consistency
- Airtight container, for storage

DIRECTIONS

1. Using the skills you learned in Chapter 1, cut and bake heart-shaped cookies.

If you haven't figured it out by now, I am a little bit obsessed with pink. So although conversation heart candies are more of a pastel palette, I chose to stick to reds and pinks! Customize these to your taste. The nice part about the color palette I chose is that I was able to use the skills from the pumpkins in Chapter 6 and mix all the similar colors in the same bowl. I used "Pink" ProGel to create the two shades of pink, adding in more pink color the second time around to create the darker shade. Finally, I mixed in AmeriColor "Super Red" to create the red shade. Keep in mind that your colors will dry about a shade darker, so all of your colors should be a shade lighter during the process of mixing.

2. Pipe and flood all of the hearts in the various shades, and let them set before adding text. I would recommend cookies sit anywhere from 30 minutes to an hour before adding the additional detail.
3. Next, add your message!

Let's talk text. Nice handwriting doesn't translate to perfectly scripted cookies. Writing with a piping bag is a completely different skill than working with any other medium. Here are a few tips to get you started.

Always find the center of the text you plan on adding to the cookie before you start piping. Working from the center out will ensure even spacing and plenty of room for the entire word. Trust me, running out of space happens!
XO

- When you begin, keep in mind it is easiest to write in capital block letters. Start with simple words such as “LOVE,” “BFF,” “CUTIE,” and “XOXO” to get you going.
- Write out what you plan to say first, and then locate the center letter or space; this will be your starting point.
- Important: instead of working from left to right, start from the center and work outwards.

Refer to the “cutie” cookie in the photo. “T” is the center letter, so I piped the “T” first and then worked my way outwards on either side. This ensures that you won’t run out of space and that you will have the correct spacing overall. Eventually you will graduate from this technique and write left to right, but until then, find your center! No shame in the practice game. To this day, I take text on a trial spin on some parchment paper before committing it to a cookie. You have to make sure the mojo is right!

Added text or not, these chubby hearts are pretty cute! Text can be one of the stickiest skills to hone. Don't be shy about practicing on parchment paper before you dive into the cookies. The more you practice, the better the results!

4. Finish adding text to all of your hearts. How did you do? My guess is you're probably a little frustrated. This skill is *hard*, and it is nothing to be ashamed of. Your friends won't care what the text looks like once they've taken a bite, and if it really bothers you, you can eat them all yourself! Please don't get discouraged, and keep practicing on that paper!

Can I let you in on a secret? Projectors are commonly used in decorating to get those perfect lines and to create logos and so on. Yes, I said projectors; are you thinking about those traumatizing school years when your teacher used one? It is the same concept, but the projection is pointed down onto a cookie. I don't dive into using a projector in this book because you might slam the book down in protest if I tell you there is another piece of equipment you need. Although it's true, you may need one, just not for the purposes of this book!

•

The love chapter is coming to a close. This is probably my favorite chapter and set of skills to learn and practice, although I might suggest giving your single friends a heads-up before they read it so they don't end up drinking the alcohol instead of decorating cookies.

Notes

- Check out Chapter 12 to see a unique way to display cookies at your next event! Hint: There is one for everyone!
- If you discover adding text to cookies is your jam, branch out and try different fonts and longer sayings. Valentine's Day is my favorite time of year to add cheeky sayings!

Chapter 9

Birthday – Celebration

It's a party, and we're here to have fun! To the majority of the population, this would be considered the birthday chapter. However, if you know me, you know I love any excuse to celebrate, so I wanted to include a few designs that can work for any mini party you're having. Before you ask, yes, we are making cookies that look like a cake. Although if you're celebrating something, I hope you get to celebrate with both cookies *and* cake, because hey, it's all about you, and I think you deserve both treats because life is short. Not to mention that making cookies look like other foods is irrationally cute, so I had to share the cuteness.

Birthday Cake Cookies

INGREDIENTS

- Birthday cake-shaped cookies
- Sprinkles
- Piping bag, number 30 tip
- Airtight container, for storage
- Icing in pink (recommended), white, orange, and yellow, in both pipe and flood consistencies

DIRECTIONS

1. Per the instructions in Chapter 1, cut out and bake your birthday cake cookies. To add an extra level of flair, mix 1 cup of sprinkles into your dough.

Nothing says a party like biting into a cookie stuffed with sprinkles! This won't change the flavor of the cookie, just add a little extra party pizzazz to it. I adore these single candle cookies because what you're celebrating is a little vague. Is it a first birthday? An 80th? A graduation?

They add an air of mystery, and let's be honest, it's a great cutter to have around because you can use it for everything.

Your colors will help set the tone for the celebration, so pick accordingly. You will see I chose warm brown for a chocolate cake and pink for details. When making the icing for the cake, you will need both pipe and flood consistencies. You will also need additional icing in piping consistency to fill a piping bag with a number 30 tip. Refer to Chapter 6 if you need to refresh on how to add a tip to the bag. You will also need white, orange, and yellow in pipe and flood consistencies for the candle.

2. Cake time! Pipe and flood the base of your cake with your color of choice.
3. While the icing on the cake is setting, pick a complementary color for the candle. For example, I chose a pink candle on a chocolate cake and a white candle on a pink cake. You will only need a piping consistency for the candle icing; start perpendicular to the cake at the bottom on the candle and move in a tight looping motion, overlapping your lines until you reach the top. This

is to give the candle a wax texture; feel free to go your own route here if you prefer a different look.

4. To create a realistic flame, you will need to pick at least three colors. In this case, the flame is so small that three is perfect. If you were to decorate a campfire cookie, more than three colors may look best.
5. Pipe around the edge to create your dam with your darkest color, orange. Using your flood icing, follow the piped line only—do not fill in completely!
6. Using the next darkest color, yellow flood icing, fill in the rest of the candle so no cookie is exposed.
7. Finally, with the lightest shade, white, add a dot of white at the base of the flame on top of the yellow.
8. Take your needle tool and mix all three colors a bit to give the appearance of a flame. Make sure to work quickly here. All the colors need to be wet for this to work. The best part of flames is that they're all different, so don't get too stuck on this process; everyone will get the idea that it's a flame.
9. Pick up your piping bag with the number 30 tip. In a looping motion, slowly add the puffy detail on the bottom of the cake. It can be a game time decision

whether to add sprinkles or not. If you are not happy with how your added detail turned out, throw some sprinkles on it to cover any mistakes.

Voilà! The easiest cake you ever did decorate. There is no flame warning either, it's completely edible! Make sure you allow enough time for cookies to dry overnight or for about 8 hours before any partying occurs.

•

Next up in party supplies are the balloons, except these will save you a tank of helium. There is a "wet on wet" technique that is super popular and versatile. We touched on it a little bit with the flame on the candle, but now we'll go into it in a bit more depth. Wet on wet technique means that you are adding a different color of flood icing onto your flooded cookie for added detail of light glare, different patterns such as dots, and more advanced things, like eyes on characters. We will be adding a light glare to give the balloons an added sense of depth and a rounded look.

Balloon Cookies

INGREDIENTS

- Balloon-shaped cookies
- Needle tool
- Airtight container, for storage
- Icing in white and other desired colors, both pipe and flood consistencies (ProGel's "Tangerine" color is recommended to recreate the pictured cookies)

DIRECTIONS

1. Cut out and bake your balloon cookies from the instructions in Chapter 1. The colors you choose for the balloons are up to you! You will need both pipe and flood consistencies in all the colors you do choose as well as white flooding. For reference, I used "Tangerine" ProGel to create the orange you see in the photo. I do not recommend making white balloons because the added detail will not show up.

2. Pipe and flood your balloons in your desired colors. Immediately after you put down your flood piping bag for a cookie, pick up the white flood bag and add a single dot to the top left edge of the balloon.
3. Using your needle tool, insert the tip into the center of the dot, and in a downward sweeping motion, drag your tool along the edge of the balloon.
4. Repeat steps until your white glare is to desired proportions.
5. Allow cookies to dry about 8 hours before serving; store in an airtight container.

•

So, your balloons and cake are ready, but your celebration is BIG and you need to really impress. Take your newly learned text skills from the previous chapter and pipe a simple message on the cake! "Happy Birthday" is my most piped phrase ever, so take your time to learn it. Type out "Happy Birthday" in different fonts and sizes and spend a few minutes tracing the letters to gain some muscle memory.

The simplest light glare detail is just the added touch that balloons need for visual interest. Immediately after the white dot is added to the wet base, use your needle tool to drag in a sweeping motion following the shape of the balloon. The white icing will follow your motion. Repeat until you are pleased with the glare.

Are you ready for the most impressive idea yet? Your guests' minds will literally explode. Decorate a cake with your cookies!!! Yep, you heard that right. Buy a cake, because let's be real, you don't have time to decorate cookies AND a cake! Stand the cookies up along the base of the sides of the cake—the frosting will act as a glue to hold the cookies up. Smaller cookies make the most adorable cupcake toppers.

Throw some sprinkles around, because it's a celebration, after all!!

Notes

- A light glare detail is not just for balloons. Anything with a natural shine, such as a bottle or a car, can benefit from the small impactful details. Typically, all glares are made with white icing.

Chapter 10

Baby Theme

Oh, baby, baby! If there is one way to celebrate a newborn, it is with cookies. They're the whimsical touch every party needs and can be made to match any theme! I love using onesies because they are a blank canvas and also give off baby vibes for all of those cool moms out there. The latest trend we're seeing with baby-themed cookies is sip 'n' sees! People are favoring parties after the baby is born where the guests can sip champagne, see the new parents, and view the beautiful new baby. I just love this sweet tradition, and anytime you can appropriately sip champagne in the afternoon, count me in. For the purposes of hammering the baby theme home, I went with the traditional blue and pink colors—like you thought I would pass up a pink opportunity?! But I have to say I am really enjoying the creative baby themes that are going beyond any traditional colors and themes.

In this chapter we'll go over how to make "wet on wet" dots for the fan favorite polka dot background, and we'll also break out a tip to create a ruffle. I decided to teach you these techniques on onesies because they are both super sweet details. Also, once you nail them, all your cookies will be dotting and ruffling!

Pop the bubbly, it's a gender reveal party! I love the mix of pink and blue to keep an air of mystery for the party guests trying to guess.

Baby Onesie Cookies

INGREDIENTS

- Onesie-shaped cookies
- 1 piping bag of your ruffle color in a pipe consistency with a number 45 tip in place
- Icing in shades of pink and blue, respectively, in both pipe and flood consistencies (ProGel "Pink" and "Baby Blue" are recommended)

DIRECTIONS

1. Cut and bake your onesie cookies per the instructions in Chapter 1.

As mentioned above, you will need both pipe and flood icing in white and two shades each of pink and blue. I used small amounts of ProGel "Pink" and "Baby Blue" to achieve the bright colors in the photos. You will also need a piping bag of your ruffle color in a pipe consistency with a number 45 tip in place. For those of you who are all about the tipless bags (like myself), this is the last tip I will reference. In my opinion, the three specialty tips mentioned throughout the book are all you will ever need to decorate your cookies. That doesn't mean others aren't important or convenient to have around, just that these three will get the task done. Now, before any of you cookie pros interject and tell me you can make ruffles with a tipless bag, it's true, you can make ruffles with a tipless bag; *but* I find it difficult and a little messy at times, so for the purposes of learning, let's go with a tip!

2. Pipe and flood the base of the baby girl onesies. Allow cookies to set before adding the seam details onto the edges; I like to pipe them in a different color so they really pop. Due to the weight of the ruffle, allow the cookies to continue to dry before adding the final detail.
3. Pick up your piping bag containing the tip and give it a squeeze to make sure all the icing is coming out evenly. Starting at the waist of the onesie (do babies have waistlines?!), hold the piping bag perpendicular over the onesies, making sure the flat side of the tip is parallel to the cookie. Starting at the top of the waistline, make contact with the cookie with your icing and slowly

move your piping bag down as far as you want to make the ruffle extend, in this case, to the top of the leg opening.

4. Keeping your tip in the exact same position, slowly bring it back to the top, continuously repeating this motion in a wave pattern as you move across the cookie left to right.
5. Set aside the tray to dry overnight.

Everyday I'm ruffling! You will be adding ruffles all year long. Ruffle piñata? Check. Ruffle pumpkins? Check. Ruffle Santa Claus? I mean, why not! Play around with your number 45 tip to get different versions of ruffles. Ruffles belong on everything, not just the future ballerinas in your life.

Back to this "wet on wet" stuff: I'm here to let you in on the secret of making perfectly smooth polka dots on all your cookies! This is definitely one of the most utilized techniques. It truly can be added to any design; a holiday doesn't pass where polka dots aren't present.

White polka dots are my favorite due to the contrast, but have fun with different colors. Are ruffles the yin to the polka dots yang? You decide.

6. Hopefully you saved enough onesies for some dots! Pipe the outline of the onesie in your preferred color; in my case, it was the baby blue.
7. This is the hardest step to master, so read it to the end before you give it a whirl. You will need to flood your cookies with your base color, however, it is not with the normal amount of flood icing. Keep in mind that each dot you will be adding is adding volume to your flood base; too much volume will cause your icing to flow over the piped edge dam and onto the cookie sheet, leaving your dots looking like melting blobs instead of perfect circles. To avoid excess volume, flood the base of the onesie with about *half* the amount of icing you would typically use. The needle tool can be used to spread icing around. Your base will look thin and uneven, but do not stress.
8. Using white flood icing, immediately squeeze even amounts onto the uneven base in a symmetrical pattern. The dots may look like little mounds at first but will eventually settle. Feel free to give the cookies a small shake to help

with the leveling process. The addition of dots should bring the volume of the flood icing to a normal level of puffiness. The end. Give it a try!

One of the most surprising parts, something that still gives me trouble from time to time, is the most methodical way to add the dots. The best advice I can give is to work in rows, alternating odd and even numbers of dots per row.

9. Once your polka dot bases have set, pipe the seam detail in an alternate color; I chose a dark blue. This is the time to add any additional detail you want to customize your cookies for your event. I would suggest a monogram or a simple bow tie for additional details.
10. Let cookies dry overnight or for about 8 hours depending on your location, then store in an airtight container until you're are ready to celebrate.

Tip #45 will be used to create a ruffle on the onesies. There are different variants of techniques on how to create the ruffle, so take a minute to play around with different styles on parchment paper. Finally, don't forget: just because your bag is disposable, it does not mean that the tip is! Don't throw away your metal tip!

When creating cookies for baby showers, it can be easy to overload on the cuteness and lose your focus on your overall theme. My first question when working with clients in the design process is to ask for a copy of the invitation, not because I plan on showing up to the party, but because it is the best way to create a focus for the cookie designs. What stands out on the invite? It could be anything from the colors to the fonts or even special characters and designs. If the whole invitation is blue, you'll be sure to match the cookies to the color scheme. This tip applies to any sort of party, not just those in the baby realm. It is easy for party throwers to get overloaded with photos these days, and you taking a look at their invitation will help you to narrow down what they are looking for without them asking you to replicate designs they have already seen somewhere else. Happy designing!

Notes

- This chapter refers to the third and final icing tip I have suggested for you to purchase. To recap, tip numbers 18, 30, and 45 have all been utilized. These are not absolutely necessary purchases in order to create beautifully decorated cookies, but I highly recommend experimenting with specialty tips as you gain better skills.

Chapter 11

Holiday

When most people think of decorated cookies, they think of Christmas. Although that may be reasonable, I have a whole business that proves decorated cookies are popular and festive all year long. Nevertheless, Christmas cookies still reign supreme, and we churn out more Santa Claus cookies than I can count. I originally created these simple Santa faces as a way to quickly turn out Mr. Claus during our busiest month of the year but later came to appreciate its simplicity; you will apply the same principles we go over in this chapter to different character cookies.

Eyes are hard. I said it. It's hard to create that perfect cartoon eye, and before you know it, you'll have a tray of cookie faces with hundreds of eyes looking at you. Trust me, nightmares may occur! I wanted to teach you these Santa faces to show you that even though there are no eyes, no one will doubt that it is a Santa Claus cookie.

These are the most in-depth cookies in the book. Please refer to the photos of the Santa in sequential order. Keep in mind Santa Claus is coming to town no matter what your cookies look like, so don't let this be an added stress during the holiday buzz. Have some eggnog and buckle up. North Pole, here we come!

Santa Claus Cookies

INGREDIENTS

- Santa face-shaped cookies
- A batch of Royal Icing
- Needle tool
- Airtight container, for storage
- Icing in AmeriColor's "Bright White," "Super Red", and "Copper (Flesh Tone)," in both pipe and flood consistencies

DIRECTIONS

1. Cut and bake off your Santa faces. These principles can be applied to a variety of Santa face cookie cutter shapes. Let cookies cool completely on the tray, rearrange the cool cookies to the outer edge of the tray for easier decorating.
2. Make a batch of Royal Icing. You will need both pipe and flood in "Bright White," "Super Red" and "Copper (Flesh Tone)." All of these colors are AmeriColor gels. Use a very small amount of copper mixed with warm brown; the amount is dependent on what skin tone you are trying to achieve.

Always keep your copper to a minimum—Santa does not need a spray tan. Remember that icing dries a shade darker, so your red should look about a shade lighter than your desired final shade. Mix colors and fill piping bags, cutting the standard amount off the tip for both the pipe and flood bags.

3. To keep all your Santa faces uniform, work in the same order on each cookie, starting at the top. Outline the hat in red. Pipe a circle in white for the puffy ball, and add a white band to fill in later as the fur trim. Still using white piping, add a semi-circle for the face at the bottom of the fur trim gap. Finally, outline the beard at the edge of the cookie to complete the piping.

For reference, this is the first cookie on the left, and each step from now on will move one cookie to the right.

This chapter covers
in-depth step-by-step
instructions to accompany
this progression shot. Refer
to this photo for a visual
explanation.

4. Flood the hat in red and the semi-circle in your skin tone icing color, using your needle tool to fix any blemishes. You are able to flood these at the same time; since they are not touching, you do not run the risk of blurring the lines. Let the flood icing set.

5. Once the skin tone icing is set, flood the beard in white. We want the fur trim to have some texture, so instead of filling in the trim with flood consistency, we are going to use pipe! Yes, pipe! Starting on the top edge next to the hat, pipe in a small swirling motion all the way across, repeating in rows until the band for the fur trim is full. Use your needle tool to mix around the lines, adding more texture and breaking up any uniform lines that might have crept in. The fur band will NOT be smooth, and that is exactly the texture we are going for. Let cookies set before moving on.

6. Using the same technique from the fur trim, fill in the puffy ball with white piping icing. Attempt to add a little more icing to the ball so it stands out against the fur trim; there should be a clear difference in texture between the two. While you're still holding onto the white piping icing, draw your best mustache. Start from the center of the face covering the bottom semi-circle; this will create the illusion of cheeks. Immediately fill in the 'stache with your white flooding.

Hot cocoa and Santa
Claus make the merriest
afternoon treat! Next time you
invite your girls over for coffee,
serve your decorated cookies.
The combo is delish!

7. Final step! Once the mustache is set, use your skin tone piping bag to create a nose on the top center of the mustache. This should be a large three-dimensional dot; use your needle tool to soften any sharp edges.

Santa has come to town in seven steps! There is a lot more patience involved in letting the cookies set than technical skills used on these cookies, proving that anyone can make character cookies! Make sure the cookies are completely dry before storing in an airtight container.

•

Are you excited to include your Santa cookies on your cookie platter? What if I told you that you could also include your note to Santa, too? Behold the beauty of edible markers. I know, you're thinking we can't get through a chapter without adding another tool. Kind of true, but I believe these are a great investment and something easy to play with, not to mention that these are perfect for kiddos.

There is something special about setting out cookies and a note for Santa. We used the same plate through my entire childhood even though it only had three of the four kids' names on it, *tough luck, little sis!* We're here to start a new tradition of edible notes that Santa will love!

Cookie notes are not limited to Christmas. The added detail of the notebook makes for the perfect background for thank-you notes for teacher appreciation day. Pop a cookie note into a packed lunch for a fun surprise. Leave a cookie note by the coffee pot for an extra sweet morning. The possibilities are endless!

Christmas List Cookies

INGREDIENTS

- Rectangle-shaped cookies
- White icing, both pipe and flood consistencies
- Edible ink markers in your choice of colors
- Airtight container, for storage

DIRECTIONS

1. Per the instructions in Chapter 1, cut and bake rectangle cookies. You will only need white pipe and flood icing. If you prefer to use a color, make sure it is a light shade so the writing you'll be doing with the markers will be visible.
2. Pipe and flood the rectangles and allow to dry overnight or for around eight hours.
3. Once the cookies are completely dry, use your markers to write your message. Notice the different aesthetic of the "Dear Santa" cookies and

the note pages. We used a clean ruler to help us get straight lines without red and blue markers to resemble notebook paper. These are great to keep in the freezer in an airtight container; you can just pop them out and write a special note on them for a particularly big day. I'm pretty sure your kids will rule the lunch table.

•

Don't limit yourself to just rectangles, I would encourage you to pipe and flood any shape in white. Allow your kids to be creative and color their own Santas and jack-o'-lanterns with the edible ink markers. This is the perfect way to get them involved, especially when they aren't yet at an age to decorate with icing. I can't guarantee that you won't get a lot of curious questions about why they're allowed to color on their food. Kids say the darnedest things.

I wanted to talk about markers in the last decorating chapter because I wanted you to hone your decorating skills first instead of just working around some techniques and replacing them with marker. I regularly work with food markers but always as an added touch. Here are a few tips and ideas to utilize your markers throughout the book. Draw on the basket weave for Easter: creating each line can be tedious and messy. Markers will eliminate the frustration without sacrificing the design! The same concept applies to the ice cream cones in the summertime. Remember when I challenged you to do a mint chocolate chip ice cream design? Use markers to draw on the chips instead of making brown sprinkles. Use markers to write your birthday message on the cakes! Conversation hearts giving you trouble? Use a red marker to write out the messages. Still not ready to give up on the idea of piping your text? Draw or write your message on the cookie first and then trace marker lines with your piping bag, using them as a guide.

Start a new tradition by writing your notes to Santa right on the cookies. The only thing left on Christmas morning will be crumbs.

The holidays are such a joyous time but can lead to unnecessary stress. My hope is for you to find joy in the kitchen, either with loved ones or by baking for loved ones. Don't let the road to perfect cookies spoil any memories; trust me, people will forget the mistakes the second they take a bite. Enjoy the new tradition!

PS: It's true, you can totally nail those wet on wet Christmas trees you've been eyeing!

Notes

- The chocolate chip cookies and gingerbread men on the cookie platter are really decorated cookies! It's always fun to try to replicate food items in cookie form. This is the perfect time to blend old traditions with new. Mixing in your decorated Santas with your grandma's meringue recipe makes the treats extra special.

Chapter 12

Packaging

Drying

By now you've read the phrase "let cookies dry" approximately nine times already, but let's review. You've spent all this time baking and decorating, you don't want to ruin them on the final step! Cookies should be left out to dry in a place with good airflow. Putting trays of cookies in enclosed places like a cool oven sounds like a great idea in theory, but the lack of airflow may cause your icing to ripple during the drying process, not to mention the risk of someone turning on the oven without realizing the precious cargo is in there!

Drying time should take approximately 8 to 12 hours depending on your location. Dry climates mean a shorter drying time, while humid climates increase drying time. The royal icing layer should be completely hard all the way through. To start, I would suggest letting your cookies dry overnight and packaging first thing in the morning. If you notice your cookies seem stale, which should never be the case, consider making the drying time shorter. Luckily for your loved ones, checking for freshness is a job for your taste testers!

Storing

Make sure you are storing the cookies in an airtight container; a plate with foil over the top is not going to cut it. We package all of our cookies individually in cellophane bags, which ensures each cookie stays fresh for about two weeks. To seal the bags, if you don't own a heat sealer, which I am assuming the majority of you do not, tie a ribbon to close the bag tight. For those of you wanting to gift your cookies, this is the final touch for a polished look.

Presentation

Showcase your new skills by bringing a party platter of cookies to your next party. Individually wrapped cookies are perfect, especially since guests can slip them into their pockets for a treat on their way home, but don't always give that wow factor. Arrange unwrapped cookies on a tray immediately before serving to ensure freshness. Trays with 4 to 8 designs are the most visually appealing.

Bridal shower? Use ribbon to tie an engagement ring cookie to a bottle. For a centerpiece that is sure to impress, align six bottles with coordinating ribbons and cookies. Hosting a brunch? Fill classic dairy jugs with milk and add a sturdy straw to each, then hang any cookie design with a hole off of the straw. Ring and donut cookies will be the most impressive cookies and milk your guests have ever seen!

Now, this next suggestion is intended to utilize all your new skills. Add names or messages by piping or writing with edible markers on all your favorite designs. Place cookies on each place setting at the table to welcome guests or direct them where to sit. Trust me, most people will be having dessert as a first course that day!

Notes

- There are many fun ways to get creative with cookies after they're complete, so don't let your creativity stop. Show off your new skills! Post pictures on social media and take pride in all your hard work! Most importantly, don't forget to tag us with the hashtag *#acookietocelebrate* so we can see!

Cellophane bags
are a great way to
individually package
cookies and keep them
fresh. Seal the bags
with a tight bow.